Introduction for parents, teachers and friends

Questions, questions, questions! Children are full of questions:
Why is peanut butter sticky? Where do raindrops go? Why do I
have four fingers and a thumb? Why is grandma's hair gray?
What do cats think? How do words get through the telephone?
Can I ride on a cloud? Questions show that a child is thinking;
they are a wonderful avenue to learning.

   We must treat a child's questions with respect—even the silly
questions. Some of them reach toward profound truths. For
example a five-year-old will ask with a giggle, "Can God see in
the dark?" We could pass the question off with a laugh or a
quick answer and change of subject. But the question reaches to
the very nature of God; it searches out his power, his knowledge. In more lofty tones, the psalmist asked the same question
in Psalm 139: "Where can I flee from your presence? . . . even
the darkness will not be dark to you."

   This book is based on questions, a child's questions: *Who is
God? Who is Jesus? What is a Christian? What Happens When
we Die?* (Lifelong students of theology ask the same questions.)
This book treat these questions with respect, provides biblical
answers shaped in a child's language with illustrations from a
child's experience. Read with your child stopping often to
explain, discuss, listen to more questions, ask questions of your
own. Notes at the end of each section will help you review
basic concepts and continue talking together. Take time to cud-
dle and play along the way. You can even add a few words of
prayer. Whether you are a parent, teacher, or friend of a child,
you can deepen your faith and grow together in the knowledge
and experience of God.

Blessings,
Carolyn Nystrom, 1998

Children's Bible BASICS

QUESTIONS KIDS ASK ABOUT BELIEF

by Carolyn Nystrom
ILLUSTRATED BY EIRA B. REEVES

Who is God?
Who is Jesus?
What is a Christian?
What Happens When we Die?

Who Is God?

Who is God?
I think and think but mostly I think of questions, because God is not like anyone or anything that I know.

—Can God hear me pray if someone else talks to Him at the same time?

—How can I hear God talk?

—Did God make my toys?

—Will God hurt me?

—What does God look like?

—Can I love God and fear Him t

4

—Does God speak English? or Spanish?

Can God see in the dark?

—Does God wear clothes?

—Does God love me?

—Where does God live?

—Does God know what I think?

5

I know my grandma because I hear her voice on the phone. I know this caterpillar because I feel him walk down my finger. I know my mom because she hugs me and reads me stories—and besides, she looks different from other mothers.

But how can I know God? I have never seen Him or touched Him, and I never heard Him speak.

God is so wise and so wonderful that we cannot know everything about Him. Our minds are not strong enough. But God wants us to know some things about Himself. So He chose certain people to write a book about Him. It is called the Bible.

7

Everyone in my family looks different. My sister Grace has little feet. My daddy has glasses. My baby brother has a fat tummy. And my mom looks most like herself when sitting cross-legged on the floor.

What does God look like?

The Bible says that no one has seen God because God is a spirit. That means He doesn't have a body at all. God simply doesn't "look like." But we can know what kind of person God is because for a while Jesus, God's Son, was a man. Then He had a body like ours.

John 14:16, 26

But Jesus is God, and He prayed to His Father to give the Holy Spirit. That makes three. How can God be three persons and only one God?

That is a mystery called the Trinity—one of the things our minds can't totally understand about God.

A yardstick has a beginning and an end. It measures how tall I am. I begin at my feet and I end at my head. My life begins and ends too. I was born as a baby, I will live for a while, then I will die. Everyone does.
Does God?

No. God is the only person who never began and never will end. God is. He always was and always will be. Not only that, God never changes. He never has and He never will.

I don't know anyone else who doesn't change at all—at least sometime.

I am learning to read. But my daddy knows more than I do. He teaches college students. Sometimes he studies books. He says the writers of those books know more than he does. And I suppose someone else taught the writers. How much does God know?

God knows all things. God never needed to learn because He knew it all in the beginning. Even the smartest person in the world does not know as much as God.

Once my mom was feeding my baby brother. But I wanted her to fix my plane right away. So I yelled, "Mom, come help me now."

Mom kept right on feeding my brother. She said, "Jimmy, I can't be in more than one place at a time."

Can God?

God is everywhere—all the time. He doesn't have to fly fast from one place to another. He just *always is everywhere*. No matter where we are, God is with us.

I like that.

What is the most powerful thing in the world?
I asked a lot of people. Is it a lion? Is it a king? Is
it a huge coal-mining machine? Is it a bomb?
Is God more powerful than these?

God is more powerful than anything or anyone. He can do anything He chooses. God made the sky and the stars—even those we can't see. He made the whole world and everything in it. Then He called it all good. But God didn't go away. God still takes care of everything that He made—
even us.

Did God make my plane?
No, but God created people and made them able to make my plane.

Some days I wake up and say to myself, "Today I'm going to be good all day. I'm going to help mother with the baby, I'm going to stay out of fights, and I'm not going to say even one naughty word."

But I always forget by supper. I'm just not perfect. Is anyone? Is God?

Psalm 18:30; Isaiah 6:1–5

God is not only perfect, He is more than perfect. He is holy. God has never done wrong. He has never made a mistake. Even His plans are perfect. Because God is perfect in every way, we can't quite imagine Him. He is so different from us. But God wants us to try to be like Him —as much as we are able. This pleases Him.

21

I like things fair. If Grace gets a piece of candy, I want one too. I get angry if a friend rides my bike without asking, or if someone at school grabs a book that I saw first. A grown-up usually straightens this out, but sometimes what she decides doesn't seem quite right. Is God always fair?

Deuteronomy 32:4; Romans 14:10–12

Because God is perfect in every other way, God is also perfectly fair. The Bible says that someday God will judge the whole world—every person who has ever lived.

I'm glad I'll have a fair judge. I know God won't make any mistakes.

Everyone I know gets angry. Grace gets mad if I sneak up and pull her hair, even if I'm just playing. Mom doesn't like it if I'm late for breakfast. My teacher gets angry if I talk while she is talking. Is God ever angry?

Proverbs 6:16–19; Matthew 22:37–40; Romans 3:23; 1 John 1:9

Because God is holy, He hates all sin. God does not want us to do anything that shows we do not love Him or that hurts another person. And God must punish sin. But God wants us to tell Him we are sorry when we do wrong. Then He will forgive us and help us do right next time.

My daddy is in charge of my family. He works so that we can have food and a house and toys. He and Mom decide when I will go to school and where we will go to church and whether we will buy a new car. They take care of me. But I have to do what they say. If I don't, there is fast trouble. Being in charge of a family is a big job. Is anyone in charge of the whole world?

1 Chronicles 29:11–13; Psalm 8:3; Matthew 10:29

God is. Because God created the world and the heavens and the stars and the planets, God can be in charge of them too. The Bible says He holds the stars in place but He cares even when a sparrow falls to the ground. God is in charge of people too—each of us.

I'm glad God is so wise and strong and holy. I wouldn't want anyone less than God to have that kind of control.

27

I know lots of nice people. But none of them is good all the time. Even my best friend lied when he said he didn't have my red crayon. Later, I saw him using it, and I knew that crayon was mine. Is God like that?

No, God is good all the way through.

29

John 15:15

When I think of all these truths about God, I can almost feel my head stretching. But the Bible says something else about God. It says God loves His people. He calls them "friends."

Exodus 15:11–13

So I worship God. I say, "God, You are wonderful. Thank You for letting me know You. I love You."

31

God loves me too.
He is my friend.

More questions to talk about

Who is God?

What do you wonder about God?

Can God see in the dark? Why?

Where is God?

Who is in charge of the whole world?

Can God hear you pray if someone else is praying at the same time? Why?

How can we hear God talk?

Does God ever do anything wrong? Why?

How is God different from you?

Does God love you? How much?

A Bible story to read and talk about:
Genesis 1:1-2:3; Psalm 139

Who Is Jesus?

I have a special friend.
Let me tell you about Him.
His name is
Jesus.

Long long ago, before there was a world or a star or even a sky, there was Jesus. Together with God, His Father, and God the Spirit, Jesus made the world. He made all the big trees and tiny flowers, and all the animals—the funny rhinoceros and the gentle puppy.

God made the sky and everything in it. Then God made people—a man and a woman. The man and woman loved each other and together they loved God. Jesus loved them too. He walked and talked with them every day.

But one day the man and woman did something wrong. They did not obey God. That is sin. Because God is holy, He could no longer walk and talk with them. So the man and woman had to leave the beautiful place God had made for them. After that they worked hard digging up stones and briars to plant seeds for food. They were often tired and hungry. They had children, and their children sinned too.

But God still loved them. He promised that one day He would send Someone to take away sin.

39

Isaiah 53:4–6; Micah 5:2

Thousands of years passed. The world filled with people. They all sinned. But over and over God sent men called prophets to remind the people of that special Someone who would make them once again right with God.

Then Jesus came.

God sent His own Son to earth, not as a powerful king but as a tiny baby. God gave Jesus a mother named Mary, but God was His Father. Jesus grew inside Mary's tummy just like other babies. He was born like other babies.

God knew that Jesus would need a daddy to take care of Him while He was growing up, so Mary's husband, Joseph, became His adopted daddy.

I like my family. I'm glad Jesus had a family too.

Mary and Joseph had to take a long trip to Bethlehem just before Jesus was born. When they got there, Joseph looked hard for a place to sleep, but the town was crowded with other travelers. There was no room left. Finally they found a cave where cows and donkeys stayed. That night Jesus was born. Mary wrapped her new baby in warm cloths and laid Him in a manger to sleep.

Later that night something wonderful happened in a field not far from Bethlehem. Shepherds were watching their sheep. Suddenly a brilliant light filled the sky, and angels appeared. They told the shepherds that Jesus, the Savior God had promised long ago, was now born. They even told the shepherds where they could find Him in the nearby town. Then the angels shouted praises to God and disappeared into heaven.

The shepherds hurried to see the new baby. They were Jesus' first visitors.

Luke 2:41–52; Mark 6:3

Jesus grew up like other boys in His town. He studied God's Word, the Old Testament Bible. He visited God's house, the Temple. He obeyed His parents. He learned to build with wood because that was His adopted daddy's job. So Jesus became a carpenter.

I wonder if Jesus liked to work with His daddy. I do.

Because Jesus was like other children, He had feelings just like I do. He felt happy when He played with pebbles in the warm sun. He felt sad when friends were mean to Him. When He fell down and skinned His knees, they hurt—just like mine.

But Jesus was also different from other boys. He was God. He never sinned. Even when Satan, God's greatest enemy, came to Jesus and tried to talk Him into doing wrong, Jesus said no. He remembered what He had studied in the Bible. That helped Him say no to Satan.

Jesus grew up to be a man. Then He looked like other men in His part of the world. There, most men had light brown skin and dark hair. They grew their hair and beards long. They wore long loose robes to protect them from the sun and sandals to make it easier to walk over the sandy soil. Jesus walked hundreds of miles so He may have carried a walking stick to help when He got tired. Probably He wrapped a wet turban around His head to keep Him cool on scorching sunny days.

For three years, Jesus walked up and down His country. He crossed sandy deserts and climbed rocky hills. He traveled across lakes in a small boat. He visited small towns, big cities, and wild empty places in the country. Everywhere, people followed Him.

The people wanted Jesus to teach them. So He taught them what He knew from studying the Bible. But He also taught them more. Jesus was God's Son. He had lived with God His Father, since before the world began. So Jesus taught the people to know God.

He taught them how to pray to God, how to please God. And He taught them how to live together without hurting each other.

John 6:1–14

Once, more than five thousand people followed Jesus to a lonely place to hear Him teach. The people were tired and hungry from the long walk.

Jesus felt sorry for them. Maybe He was tired and hungry too. He asked if anyone had food to share. Only one small boy brought his lunch to Jesus. Jesus prayed, thanking His Father for the food. Then slowly He began to break the boy's bread and fish into small pieces. And the most amazing thing happened. More and more pieces came from the boy's lunch, but Jesus did not run out of food. Jesus' friends passed out bread and fish to the people. They all ate until they were full, even the little boy. Even then, the food was not gone. Twelve basketfuls were left over.

I wonder how that boy felt when he saw his lunch feeding so many people. I wonder if he knew that Jesus had made the whole world, so it would be no trouble to make his lunch into a little extra food.

Sometimes sick people crowded around Jesus, and He helped them. Jesus made clay for a man who couldn't see from the time he was a baby. He put it on the man's eyes. When the man washed his eyes, he could see.

Friends carried a man who couldn't move at all to see Jesus. Jesus spoke to him, and the man picked up his mat and walked away.

A woman who had been sick for twelve years touched Jesus' clothing, and Jesus made her well.

A twelve-year-old girl died. Jesus came to her house and brought her back to life.

Mark 10:13–16

Once a group of children came to Jesus. His friends told the children that Jesus was tired and they should go away. But Jesus reached out His arms to them and took them on His lap.

I'm glad Jesus takes time for children because I need a lot of time.

But not everyone loved Jesus. Bad men were afraid of Him because they did not want to change their lives to please God. They were afraid of the big crowds who followed Jesus. So they made up lies about Jesus and told those lies to the governor. Together they decided that Jesus must die. So soldiers nailed Jesus' hands and feet to a cross. That was the way they killed people who disobeyed important laws.

But Jesus hadn't done anything wrong. Because He is God, He could have come down from the cross if He had wanted to. But He didn't.

I am sad when I think how Jesus died, but I am thankful too—because He did it for me.

John 3:16; Romans 10:9–10; 2 Corinthians 5:21

   You see, every person in the world has done wrong—even me. Sometimes no one sees my sin, like the time I took my sister Ruth's candy and hid it in my closet. But God knows. And my sin makes Him sad. It makes me sad too. I thought of other things I had done wrong, and I worried that God would punish me.

Then I remembered, *That's why Jesus died. He took the punishment for my sin.* So I prayed, "Jesus, I'm sorry I did wrong. Thank You for taking my punishment. I want to be Yours from now on."

And God forgave me. I am His child for ever and ever.

(I knew Jesus would want me to give Ruth back her candy—so I did, even before she asked.)

57

After Jesus died on the cross, Jesus' friends were sad and frightened. Some went back to work, others ran away. But three days later something wonderful happened.

Jesus came back alive!

For many days He walked and talked with His friends. They could touch Him. Once Jesus even cooked breakfast for them. He taught them to understand the Bible better than they ever had before. Then one day Jesus gathered His friends together. While they were all watching, Jesus was lifted straight up into heaven.

Romans 8:34; Hebrews 7:25

Do you wonder what Jesus does in heaven? He hears and answers prayers—the prayers of all His people on earth (mine too).

John 14:1–7

And He is making heaven ready for us to come and live with Him. I can't imagine what heaven is like, but if Jesus makes it for me, I know I'll like it.

1 Thessalonians 4:13–18

But the best part of Jesus' story hasn't happened yet. Jesus is coming back to earth! All of us who love Jesus will be caught up to meet Him in the air. Even people who have died will come back to life, just as He did.

And we shall live with Jesus in heaven for ever and ever.

Jesus is my special friend, but He is much more than a friend; He is my God.

So I pray to Him.

I try to do what is right, because I know Jesus wants me to.

I thank Jesus for dying for me.

Even when I'm sad, I remember, *Jesus loves me.* And I feel warm and snuggly inside.

Jesus loves you too. He wants to be your friend. Why don't you ask Him?

More questions to talk about

Who is Jesus?

Where was Jesus when the world began?

What special things happened when Jesus was born?

If you could be one of the people or animals around Jesus when he was born, who would want to be? Why?

Who was Jesus' Father? Explain.

What did Jesus do when he was a boy?

What all did Jesus teach people?

What are some ways that Jesus helped people?

If you could sit on Jesus' lap and whisper something in his ear, what would you say?

How did Jesus die?

Why did Jesus die?

Is Jesus alive now? Where?

Where can we be with Jesus?

A Bible story to read and talk about:
Luke 2:1-20; John 14:1-4

65

What is a Christian?

Jesus is my friend.
But He is more than my friend.
I belong to Jesus.

I live with my mom and dad and my big sister, Suzy, and my baby brother, Seth. They are my family. We take care of each other and love each other.

I hold tools for my dad while he fixes the car, but Dad sits behind me and pulls on my tight boots.

I give Seth a ride on my sled, but Suzy makes me a peanut butter sandwich for lunch.

Once Suzy and I surprised Mom by setting the table for supper. We picked wild flowers for the center. But Mom cooked the supper for us.

69

People in our family belong to each other. I belong to Dad and Mom and Suzy and Seth, and they belong to me.

But I also belong to Jesus. I am in His family too. God is my Father. Jesus is my Brother. The Holy Spirit lives inside me.

God listens to me when I pray. I listen to God when I hear Bible stories. I obey God when I do what the Bible says.

I love Jesus and Jesus loves me. We belong together.

1 John 4:7, 19–5:2

And other people also belong in God's family. The people in God's family are special to each other.

When Mrs. Blake was sick, Mom took supper to her.

When Mr. Trooper lost his job, my dad felt sad. He helped Mr. Trooper find a new job.

When my friend Bobby won a spelling contest, I was almost as happy as he was. People in God's family care about each other because Jesus loves us all.

People in God's family are called Christians. I am a Christian. So are Mom and Dad and Mrs. Blake and Mr. Trooper and Bobby. It's great to have such a big family.

Because I am a Christian, God helps me to understand truths about Himself. When I saw a spider web sparkling with morning dew, I thought, *God makes beauty.* Then I noticed the spider in the corner of his web. I thought, *That spider sure isn't pretty, but God made an ugly spider able to spin a beautiful web.*

God helps me to understand the Bible too. The Bible is like a letter from God to me, so I listen carefully to stories from the Bible.

When Mom read the story of Jesus' feeding five thousand people with five loaves and two fish, I wondered, *How did Jesus do that?* Then I thought, *If God made the whole world in the beginning, then Jesus could make bread and fish to feed only five thousand people. It shows that Jesus is God.*

God helped me understand that.

God knows everything, so He knows all about me already: what I think, what I did yesterday, what I will do tomorrow, and even when I will die. But God wants me to talk to Him anyway. People in the same family talk to each other all the time, so I pray to God every day.

I told Him how much fun I had on a bike ride with Dad, and I thanked God for a sunny Saturday.

I asked God to help me fix my broken car, and soon I got the car back together.

God cares about what I do and how I feel. He wants me to ask Him for help.

When I say that I am a *Christ*ian, people know that I belong to *Christ*. The word *Christ*, another name for Jesus, is part of that name. I don't want to do anything that would cause people to think bad thoughts about Jesus. Jesus doesn't want me to do those kinds of things either. So He helps keep me from sin.

When Jesus was on earth, He never did anything wrong in His whole life. He helped people who needed help. He loved everyone, even those who were unkind to Him. He always obeyed God, His Father.

I'm not perfect, but every day Jesus is helping me live more like He did.

One day, I saw a boy roller skating. He tripped and skinned his knees. Then he sat on the sidewalk and cried. I didn't know who he was, but I asked where he lived and helped him home. Jesus would have done that too.

Another time, Butch, a tough guy at school, snatched my cap and threw it in a mud puddle. I felt awful. I wanted to hit him and kick him, do anything to make him feel as bad as I did. Later, I saw Butch's new ball with his books. I wanted to stuff it in the trash bin just to get even. But I didn't. Jesus helped me walk away.

Romans 12:17–21

The hardest part of my day is a summer evening when it is only beginning to get dark. Just when I am having the most fun playing, Mom calls me home to get ready for bed.

84

I don't want to come at all. I want to keep playing forever. But when I come on Mom's first call, it is Jesus who helps me obey.

If I come fast, we have time for a story—and I'm glad I came.

But I do not always do what Jesus wants.
Sometimes I yank toys from Seth.
I kick over Bobby's paints.
I yell, "No!" at my mom.

I feel sad after I do those things; I know that Jesus feels sad too. I say, "Jesus, I'm sorry. I'll try not to do it again."

And Jesus forgives me. He always will.

John 3:16; Romans 5:8

Jesus knows that I am not perfect. That's why He came to earth. He was perfect—even if I cannot be. So He died on a cross to take the punishment for all the things I do wrong. He invites me into His family. It's hard to understand how Jesus loves me that much. But He does.

And Jesus will never, never leave me alone. I am in His family forever.

Even now Jesus is making heaven ready for me and for all the others in His family. After we die, we will all live in heaven with Jesus. And heaven is forever.

Would you like to be a Christian? If so, you can belong to Jesus too. There are three things you need to do.

Isaiah 59:1–2; 1 John 1:9

1. *Think.* Remember the things you have done wrong. Have you ever told a lie? Taken something that was not yours? Disobeyed your mom and dad? The things that we do wrong are called sins. Any sin separates us from God.

Say, "Jesus, I'm sorry for all the things I've done wrong."

2. *Believe.* Believe that Jesus died and came back to life to forgive those sins and take them away forever.

Say, "Thank You, Jesus. I believe You took the punishment for all the things I do wrong."

3. *Decide.* Do you really want to belong to Jesus? If you do, that means that you will let Jesus be in charge of all that you do. (You will pray often. You will learn from the Bible and try as hard as you can to obey it. Whenever you do something wrong, you will tell Jesus you are sorry. And you will try to make it up to anyone that you hurt.)

Romans 12:1; John 6:35–37; Revelation 3:20

If you decide that you want to belong to Jesus, say, "Jesus, I give You myself. I want to belong to You forever."

If you take those three steps, then you are a Christian. You may not feel different, but that doesn't matter. Jesus loves you and forgives you. The Bible says that Jesus accepts anyone who comes to Him.

In God's family, there is always room.
Welcome to the family.

More questions to talk about

What is a Christian?

Who are some Christians that you know?

What are some ways that Christians take care of each other?

What does it mean to be in God's family?

Who do Christians belong to?

Why do people in God's family call themselves Christians?

Why do some people want to be Christians?

If you want to be a Christian:

What will you think about yourself?

What will you believe about Jesus?

What will you give to Jesus?

Are you a Christian? How do you know?

How are Christians different from other people?

Jesus loves you. What would you like to say to Jesus? (Tell Him.)

A Bible story to read and talk about:

John 3:1-18; Acts 16:16-34

What Happens When We Die?

Do you ever think about dying? I do.
And my thoughts are quiet, sad, scary
thoughts.

Once when I was playing in our living room, a tiny brown bird flew straight at the window. It hit the glass with a thud and fell to the ground. For a few minutes it fluttered, then it lay still. I started to cry. I wanted the bird to get up and fly again. I waited, but it didn't move, so I ran outside and picked it up. I wanted to help it fly. But the bird lay still in my hand. I yelled for Mom.

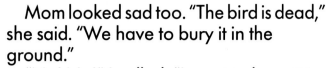

Mom looked sad too. "The bird is dead," she said. "We have to bury it in the ground."

"No! No!" I yelled. "I want to keep it in my room. Maybe it will live again."

"That won't happen," Mom said quietly.

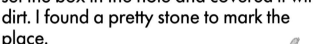

So Mom and I found a little box. We put soft cloths in the bottom. As I put the bird inside, a small feather clung to my finger. I put the feather in my pocket.

Then we dug a hole in our garden. We set the box in the hole and covered it with dirt. I found a pretty stone to mark the place.

Later, I sat holding the feather and thought long, long questions about death.

—How long does being dead last?

—Does God want people to die?

—Will my mom still be my mom in heaven?

—Will I die some day?

—Does it hurt to die?

—WHERE IS HEAVEN?

—WHY DID I HAVE TO PUT THE BIRD IN THE GROUND?

—What will happen to it there?

—Will I see the bird in heaven?

—Why do birds and animals and people die?

—How could I go to heaven if my body is in the ground?

They were hard, sad, scary questions. I cried a little for the bird that died. My mom sat beside me. She said, "It's all right to cry, Jenny." Then we talked about my questions.

Mom began by telling me again the story of God's making the world.

The world was beautiful then—perfect—with trees, flowers, animals, even little birds. Next, God made a man out of the soil of the ground. Then He made a woman out of a small bone from the man. He let the man and woman live in that beautiful place. During the day they took care of the plants and animals. In the evening God walked and talked with them. God said, "You may have everything here except one tree. If you eat fruit from that tree, you will die."

At first the man and woman wanted to obey God, but they became more and more curious about the special tree. The woman thought, *Perhaps God did not really mean what He said.* So one day she ate fruit from the tree. She gave some to her husband, and he ate too.

Romans 5:12–20; 8:18–23

The man and woman had disobeyed God; the world was no longer perfect. Ever since that time, every man, woman, plant, or animal that lives eventually dies.

But God does not want His people to be dead forever. So He sent His Son, Jesus, to make up for the wrong that first man and woman had done. Jesus lived. But He was different from any other man who lived. Jesus never disobeyed God. Then Jesus died. But His death was different too. JESUS CAME BACK TO LIFE!

When an animal dies, its body stops moving. It can't see or hear or feel anything anymore. It can't breathe. Its heart doesn't beat. At first its body may look alive even though it is quite still. But in a few days it will begin to soften and smell bad. The body slowly turns back into soil. That is why we bury dead animals in the ground.

When a person dies, the same thing happens to his body. That's why we bury it in a cemetery.

We feel sad and sometimes we cry because we feel lonely without that person who died.

But a person is more than a body. Inside is the "really me," the part that thinks and feels and loves and makes me different from any other person in the world. That is called the soul.

As soon as one of God's people dies, just as quick as you can blink your eyes, that soul goes to heaven to be with Jesus. There he can think and feel and love, and play, and even work. And he is perfectly happy, because he is with Jesus. And Jesus has made his place in heaven just exactly what that person likes best.

113

Later, God will even make his body new and take it to heaven also. It will look a little like his old body that was buried in the ground, but the new body will be perfect—just like heaven. It will not be broken or hurt or sick or ugly.

Because Jesus came to earth and died and came back to life, we can live forever in heaven with Him. And forever doesn't ever end.

When Jesus was about to die, His friends felt sad. They knew they would be lonely after Jesus was gone. But Jesus said, "Don't be sad. I am going away to make heaven ready for you. But someday I'll come back and take you to heaven with Me."

We don't know exactly what heaven is like or even where it is. The Bible says that heaven is too wonderful for our minds to understand. But it is fun to imagine what Jesus might be preparing for us. Close your eyes and try.

118

Think of the most beautiful thing you have ever seen. Was it a mountain? A field full of wild flowers? A sunset? A basketful of baby puppies? Or something totally different—something no one but you would think is beautiful?

Now open your eyes. Heaven is even more beautiful than that.

Think again. When have you felt happiest in your whole life? On a trip to the zoo? On Christmas morning? Catching raindrops on your tongue? Or sitting quietly and holding your favorite pet?

You will be happier than that in heaven.

What do you like to do more than anything else? Play football? Ride a train? Swim? Bake cookies? Swing high on a tire swing? Lie on your back in tall grass and watch the clouds?

What would you choose to do if you were able to do anything you wanted? Would you pilot an airplane? Drive a fire truck? Take care of sick animals in a pet hospital? Maybe you would fly from here to Mars and build a city there.

In heaven you will do things even more wonderful—and you will enjoy them even more.

1 Corinthians 13:8, 12; 1 John 3:2

Think of your favorite person—someone you love more than anyone else. But do you sometimes get angry and want her to leave you alone? Or do you worry that she doesn't like you as much as you like her? Do you sometimes wish you could say what you really feel to that person—only the words don't come out right?

In heaven you can know that person perfectly. She will know you too. And you will love each other all the time.

In heaven you'll meet lots of other people too. You'll know and love God's people who lived a long time before you were born—like your great-great-great-grandmother and King David and the apostle Paul. And all of you will know Jesus.

Jesus will take care of you in heaven.

"But, Mom," I asked, "will the bird that died today be alive in heaven?"

"I don't know, Jenny." Mom was quiet for a moment. "But Jesus is making heaven perfect for you. If you still want that bird when you go to heaven, I'm sure the bird will be there."

Mom left then. I sat for a while looking at my feather, but my thoughts weren't so sad and scary anymore. I think I'll keep that feather on my dresser.

More questions to talk about

What happens when we die?

Jimmy saw a bird that died when it flew against his window. Have you seen something that died? What happened?

Why are we sad when an animal or person dies?

Why do we bury a person or animal when it dies?

When you think about dying, do you get scared? Why?

When a Christian dies, what happens to the soul?

How will our new body be different than the one we have now?

Describe heaven.

How long does heaven last?

What do you think you will like best about heaven?

A Bible story to read and talk about:
1 Thessalonians 4:13-18; Revelation 21—22.

Text © 1999 by The Moody Bible
Institute of Chicago
Design © 1999 Angus Hudson Ltd/
Tim Dowley & Peter Wyart trading
as Three's Company

First published in this edition by
Moody Press in 1999.

ISBN: 0 8024 7914 6

Worldwide co-edition organized and produced
by Angus Hudson Ltd, Concorde House,
Grenville Place, London NW7 3SA
fax: +44 20 8959 3678

Printed in Singapore